About the Author

Daniel Odier was born in Geneva in 1945. He is a
novelist, screenwriter and poet, and has published over
46 works including the bestselling *Tantric Quest* (Inner
Traditions), and *Desire: The Tantric Path to Awakening*
(Inner Traditions). Anais Nin called him "an outstanding
writer and dazzling poet". The author began his studies
with Kalu Rinpoche in 1968 and remained his disciple
until his passing in 1989. In 2004, Odier received the
Ch'an ordination in the Lin t'si and Caodong schools
in China, as well as permission to teach the Zhao Zhou
Ch'an lineage in the West. Daniel taught Tantra and
Buddhism in several American Universities in 1995.
He continues to run workshops and seminars in
Europe, Canada and the United States.

The Doors of Joy

19 MEDITATIONS FOR AUTHENTIC LIVING

DANIEL ODIER

WATKINS PUBLISHING

LONDON

This edition first published in the UK and USA 2014 by
Watkins Publishing Limited
PO Box 883
Oxford, OX1 9PL
UK

A member of Osprey Group

For enquiries in the USA and Canada:
Osprey Publishing
PO Box 3985
New York, NY 10185-3985
Tel: (001) 212 753 4402
Email: info@ospreypublishing.com

1 3 5 7 9 10 8 6 4 2

Managing Editor: Deborah Hercun
Designer: Suzanne Tuhrim

Printed and bound by CPI Group (UK) Ltd, Croydon, CR0 4YY

A CIP record for this book is available from the British Library

ISBN: 978-1-78028-671-6

Watkins Publishing is supporting the Woodland Trust, the UK's leading
woodland conservation charity, by funding tree-planting initiatives and
woodland maintenance.

www.watkinspublishing.co.uk

Table of contents

Preface

D URING THE LAST TWENTY YEARS, I have taught in Europe, the United States and South America. I slowly realised that, although teaching was meant to be liberating, it was really just a repackaging of a new theory of the world. This has, in turn, created new shackles that keep human beings in a closed universe.

I discovered Zen when I was fifteen years old through the monumental writings of D.T. Suzuki. From that time on, I felt the iconoclastic power of the old Chinese masters who promoted the complete deconditioning of any belief, including Buddhism. But I was still too young to renounce an ideal system that would allow me to achieve inner peace.

Later on, I belonged to the first wave of Western invaders who hoped to discover wisdom on the roads of India. I encountered Dzogchen, personified by Dudjom Rinpoche and Chatral Rinpoche, the Vignan Bhairav Tantra, thanks to the Chinese yogi, C.M. Chen, and finally, the Vajrayana taught by the one who would become my master, Kalu Rinpoche. I followed that path for seven years and I learned a great deal from this magnificent human being who radiated total love. Little by little, the magical universe of the Tibetans felt increasingly distant from

Western thinking and I turned towards the Shaivism of Kashmir, whose philosophy, stripped of any cultural markings, touched me deeply. I met Lalita Devi, a yogini who lived as a hermit and who passed on to me the spanda and pratyabhijna ways. Her extreme, direct approach went straight to the point and avoided all spiritual traps. She knew how to debunk conditionings; by shedding light on fears, she forced one to be fearless; she destroyed the façade by giving access to spontaneity. This was not an approach I was used to learning but rather an introduction to asceticism, a renunciation of all fixations. The goal was to become a human being again, to be fully open to the world, alive and full of desire and passion, without the smallest pretension of being anything else but spontaneous.

After our separation, and faced with the implausibility of finding her again, I felt once more the attraction of Zen and entered several communities in order to deepen that practice. I had the opportunity to observe that adhering to beliefs and rules limited consciousness. I realised that systems would reconstruct themselves inside me and that this constant quest prevented all authentic liberation. The conformity and puritanism of these spiritual circles always felt too 'religious' for me. One essential ingredient was missing: joy.

While teaching, I could see how difficult it was for me not to build systems similar to those that had limited me in my quest. I could see that my students would inevitably adhere to the propensity we all have of building conceptual limitations in order to give more value to our knowledge and experience.

Over time, as I was getting closer to Chan (Chinese Zen) and to the essence of the Kashmir Shaivism, I became more and more iconoclastic, and transformed myself into a spiritual anarchist whose only ambition was to reach an authentic freedom by forgetting the path that had always been followed. I would often recall the words of Montaigne: 'I am a man and nothing that is human is indifferent to me'.

It appeared more and more evident to me that it was essential to escape any limitations and that joy was the only natural thing to reach for. The spiritual discourse seemed to me like a fatal trap. Spending time with the old Chinese masters of the Tang dynasty exposed me more and more to this bizarre freedom.

In 2005, I went to China to meet Jing Hui, the only living successor of the iconic master of the twentieth-century Hsu Yun, and I saw in him the incarnation of the freedom of the ancient philosophers. I became his disciple and eventually I was ordained a Chan master.

Since that time, free of all attachments, I venture only to help those I meet to find spontaneity, joy and freedom.

1.

Joy at the Heart of Everything

JOY OCCUPIES A CENTRAL PLACE in this quest for the absolute that is the underpinning of all life. It cannot be compared to pleasure or happiness, since these depend on external circumstances and are ephemeral. Joy is at the heart of any search, and is the clearest sign that a human being has reached the harmony derived from his philosophical, artistic and spiritual practices.

What is so special about joy is that, like any other essential element, we can always find it again. We are born with this gift, but we neglect it and seek more transient pleasures. The disappointments brought about by fleeting pleasures and the superficial idea of happiness make us forget joy, which needs constant creativity to flourish.

When one meets a joyous person, one observes that joy alone is independent of any external factor; it flourishes regardless of external circumstances and, in spite of the fact that it can fluctuate, nothing can destroy it. It is the opposite of melancholia, with its lack of connection to the circumstances of our lives. Neither the joyous nor the melancholic person needs positive or negative elements to determine their state.

One might then wonder from where this independence stems? Joy assumes a richness of connections, a multitude of factors that cancel out the destructiveness of disappointment or sadness; it is to be found at the centre of a swarm of bliss. Joy is connected to our presence in the world. It stems directly from it. To rediscover joy, we need to rediscover or develop our ability to embrace the broadest area of reality at our disposal. Joy requires practice. There are also multiple obstacles to joy that can be defeated one after the other as long as we have intuition and a clear perception of what they are.

Joy restores an innocence that comes from a bizarre wisdom: an experience of life in all its dimensions. This innocence is not ignorance of the tragic; on the contrary, it's a sharp perception of this human dynamic. One could even say that this element is inseparable from joy. Without this balance, joy would still be a fragile asset controlled by circumstances.

Authentic joy is a space where everything can become manifest, a permanent display of fireworks that does not garishly taint the sky but allows us to discover that it has no limits. Joy does not tolerate half measures. One cannot be partially joyous. When joy does not take over the whole being, it is only one of the masks of happiness. Joy implies creativity and the courage of freeing oneself from many of our own concepts and conditionings. One can only access it through steadfast fearlessness.

Examining Joy

*When I live a joyous moment, do I reconnect to other
joyous moments and to the source of joy?*

*Does the source of joy seem dependent on an object,
or is it a deeper, innate and independent feeling?*

*Does my joy depend on my presence in the world?
Does it increase in the moments when I am totally present,
or does it decrease when I am distracted or perturbed?*

*Am I under the impression that joy is conditional, depending
on the intensity of the present experiences, or does it completely
overwhelm me without any apparent reason?*

*If I made a list of events that evoke joy in me,
what would be on that list?*

On this list, how many events depend on others?

2.

Organic Joy

THE SIMPLEST JOY, THE MOST basic and essential, is organic joy. It is the first emotion felt by the child and it progressively disappears because of external influences and the anguish the child receives immediately after birth. This organic joy manifests itself powerfully during adolescence and sporadically later on. Religions negate and depreciate the body, for they see it as an obstacle to absolute purity and, therefore, they contribute to poisoning our perception of organic joy. The body becomes tense, limits its experience of the world, develops the sense that it is irreparably flawed and that it must be sacrificed for the benefit of the mind. The body gradually learns to feel alive only through pain and that, at least, gives us a sign: I suffer, therefore I am alive.

The first step towards enhancing joy consists in reconnecting with the body, accepting it, and recognising its inalienable right to life; that is, being courageous and determined to realise one's own nature. Moral injunctions will appear as a series of subtle obstacles. It will be necessary to decipher them and bring them to light. We need to listen attentively to our internal voice that constantly attempts to hinder the communication of the body with what is real. Where does this voice come from that states: You don't have the right to be alive. Is it the voice of our parents, of our teachers or of the clergy – those with whom we have rubbed shoulders? Or could it be the manifestation of our deepest fears of living life at its fullest? Or is it this famous death wish that escorts us through life? The more we listen to this voice, the more we can recognise its absurdity. It is the voice of the internal dialogue, our own voice. Therefore we can allow it to be silent. What gives meaning to life is our acceptance of being fully alive. So when death comes, we shan't regret that we did not live fully.

Once we are able to go beyond that first step, when we have given ourselves a full right to life, we will realise that our body and our capacity to feel the pulse of life and our emotions were anesthetised by years of sensory, mental and emotional deprivation. We will then realise we were given the illusion of a fragile security, ready to explode under the slightest shock.

On our road to joy, we must first abandon the very

notion of security. Life is beautiful to the extent that it is dangerous. I remember having once seen a teenager who proudly displayed a T-shirt that she had painted herself stating: 'What does not scare me is of no interest to me.' Let us remind ourselves of that courage in order to begin to taste organic joy.

Our body is a marvellous and elusive instrument. It is able to guide us in our decisions with precision and speed, thanks to its immediacy. The body only knows two words: yes and no. It does not know hesitation or indecision. Its way of saying yes is to open up, while its way of saying no is to close up. This direct message manifests itself in less than a second, while our brain is still reflecting, scanning the past, scouring statistics, establishing risks of failure, only to end up after many minutes, even hours, proposing a more prudent solution that we are very likely to adopt. Let us allow our body to operate according to its rapid mode and let us trust it in order to unblock the mind. This is our first exercise towards joy. We will be scared! We will be under the impression that we are acting foolishly! Slowly, we will rediscover the fundamental pleasure of having reconnected with our body.

By trusting the body we will rapidly develop our capacity to capture what is real. Our life will become less predictable for ourselves as well as for others. We will be astonished by the accuracy of our bodily responses and we will progressively smile at the ineffective complexity of our mental processes. Let us reserve our mind for all the marvellous things it can do and let us provide it moments when it can rest. Forcing it to work non-stop for sixteen hours a day, our mind really deserves time off. A large part of the stress and tiredness that limits us stems from the constant and incessant discourse that keeps us buzzing day and night. The body can only relax when there is silence. We are used to putting it in a state of stupor through the use of alcohol, drugs, images and sounds, when what it simply needs is to drink at the fresh fountain of silence.

Gradually, we will appreciate tasting the silence of our mind, no longer imposing the fears and boundaries that it fabricates by analysing the past. Organic joy requires the mind to be serene and tranquil. It has been of great help until this time, but we have put it to forced labour. The mind, like any other worker, deserves hours of rest. There is no labour union protecting the mind. So let us stop exerting an internal dictatorship before we revolt against the external one.

Questions for our Body

Today, what were the moments of profound satisfaction, of pleasure or of joy? Is there a difference between such moments of satisfaction and these feelings of pleasure and joy?

What is the relationship between relaxing my breathing and my internal sensations?

When I inhale, do I relax the deep muscles of the abdomen, those just above the pubic bone, or do I tighten them?

How does a baby breathe? An animal? By relaxing the stomach when I inhale or by pulling it in? Which one is natural breathing?

Being present depends on the relaxation of the breath. What would happen if I attempted to be conscious of my breath twenty or thirty times a day, for fifteen to twenty seconds?

After several days' practice, would my presence in the world begin to change?

3.

Developing Internal Silence

HOW DOES ONE DEVELOP THE silence that allows for the blossoming of organic joy? By closely observing the activity of our internal discourse and by becoming conscious of its ongoing repetitiveness. We know how to escape the drivel of everyday life, but why is it that we are completely unable to escape our internal discourse which is so predictable and boring? It is depressing to listen to this voice. We will come to realise that we are completely under the thumb of this expression of fear.

It is easy to diagnose fear. It has an immediate connection with our manifestations of hope. The more we hope, the more frightened we become. Hope is a fear that has been subverted. It signifies a lack of presence in the world, an absence of joy, a continuous search for the satisfaction of happiness. Since infinity does not ever connect with us, we seldom receive what we wished for, meaning we are constantly frustrated. When we wait continually for beauty, we become blinded to the wonders that surround us, while waiting for a fantasised happiness.

As soon as we give awareness to our body, we discover that we lack nothing we believe we need. The everyday traces of beauty are sufficient in bringing us joy. We have a body! It is capable of moving, feeling, tasting, seeing, listening and smelling the thousand perfumes of the world. Our body can also sleep, wake up, sense water spilling over the skin, it can eat, drink, walk, look at the sky, touch other human beings, make love, plunge deeply into another person's eyes, listen to music; observe a bud flowering. Bodily sensations can also migrate externally from the skin towards our internal organs. We are able to experience the fullness of the ebb and flow of blood and of other liquids. We can enjoy and appreciate our breathing, control it, allow it to get in deeper, in connection with our emotions. We can feel the movement of our diaphragm, mixing the energy of the lower body with that of the upper body. We can feel our tongue, allow it to relax, be surprised by the luminous flashes that appear on our eyeballs when the pineal gland is stimulated. The relaxation of the tongue is essential for the relaxation of the whole head.

The more we attend to what is happening inside us, the more our mind will be blessed by a well-deserved silence. It will then be in splendid form to function when we really need it. Alive and fresh, precise and creative. Overworked it will barely deliver minimal service.

Our body is able to feel the quivering of life; it can be surprised and awakened to a sense of wonder. Wonder is the surest sign of a return to organic joy.

Questions for the Mind

What do I realise when I observe the connection between the internal discourse of my mind and my frequent emotions? Am I conscious of my bodily presence?

What happens if I observe how my body is feeling while my emotions are high and what I then avoid learning from this experience?

When I share an emotion with a friend, what part does creativity play in my story?

After sharing this emotion several times, do I increase the complexity of the story by adding details that were not present the first time around?

As I become conscious of the narrative aspects of an emotion, does this bring me back to the sensation, the path of the emotion in my body. Am I aware of the tensing and relaxing of my muscles?

What is the path of an emotion inside my body? What are the sensitive points in my body that respond to different emotions?

Does concentrating only on what I feel help me to give less thought to the emotion and to its description?

9.

Freeing Oneself
of Certainties

A RE BELIEFS, DOGMAS AND CERTAINTIES an efficient way to confront reality? It would seem that since reality is fluid, the rigidity of our concepts might cause us a lot of trouble in adjusting. With this rigid functioning, we oppose a flow that ignores any other possible system. Our certainties get brushed aside by a tempest. Our lack of suppleness puts us in permanent conflict with reality.

The development of joy is directly proportional to the relinquishment of our concepts of the world. Why are we so stubbornly attached to our rigid structures? Ever since we accessed language, we have been nourished by the certainty that a system of the world is essential for our balance and happiness. The more rigid our certainties become, the more problems we have with a reality that refuses to enter into our plans.

On the contrary, would wisdom not advocate abandoning the weight of this mental machinery? This is one of the central teachings of Chinese Zen: to leave behind any conception of the world and to fully enter reality. This is the key to freedom and creativity. It is also the key to joy. When you give up the idea of having a concept of the world, there is no problem with dealing with reality since there is no mental formation giving you a signal that reality ought to be different from what it is.

How can we alleviate ourselves of our rigid concepts of the world? We need to examine carefully how our concepts create interferences, then observe how these interferences develop into conflicts that we are unable to resolve and how they add to the weight of our life, to our lack of satisfaction and to our frustrations. By an attentive examination of how we function, we can discover how ineffective this all is. When we clearly realise that this slows down our life and that we block ourselves, we will no longer challenge reality with so many concepts and we will immediately notice more fluidity in our behaviour.

This acceptance of the creativity of life is very stimulating from mental, emotional and physical standpoints. It allows us to discover that there is an immediate lesson to be discovered behind each experience, even if we give it a negative label. We also observe that no experience is completely negative. Something positive will always emerge, even in the most catastrophic of circumstances. Fukushima was a human and ecological disaster, yet we cannot deny that it helped the awakening of an acute consciousness of the danger of nuclear power and tipped the balance of some governments, such as Germany and Switzerland, towards a policy of nuclear disengagement. The breakup of a love affair may cause intense personal suffering, while at the same time allowing the emergence of a great renewal and a newly found independence.

'Men believe in something to forget who they are.
They bury themselves in ideals, get nested in idols
and kill time through the reinforcement of beliefs.
Nothing would threaten them more than to be
confronted by a pure existence that would
annihilate their pleasant self-deception.'

CIORAN

Examining Beliefs and Certainties

If I made a list of everything that is the essential frame of my life – dogmas, beliefs and certainties – what would it reveal?

If I consider each of them and try to connect them with how I act in life, would I find that they have helped me to be more congruent and more authentic?

Or are there elements in this list that create distance and separation from others?

Does my ability to listen to others change when I do not have precise information on the topic?

In an encounter, a dinner or a time of sharing, how much time is spent defending concepts?

Am I upset and troubled when someone does not share my ideas? Do I need to convince that person?

Am I able to consider that his or her concept might be as defensible as mine?

If I abandon my viewpoint, what is changed in the connection and in the way my body feels?

5.

Do We Have

a Choice?

G OING WITH THE FLOW OF life does not inhibit action. Quite the contrary, but this raises a fundamental question about choice: do we really have a choice? One of the bedrock ideas of our culture is that we have free will. Half the world defines freedom as having freedom of choice. The other half bases freedom on the absence of choice. What concept should we follow to experience freedom?

The belief in a theory complicates the matter. The old against the new will be opposite, whether one is Chinese or Western. To make it simpler, let us consider a moment when we are sure that we have made a choice. Let us take a simple example: the break-up of a love affair. When did we decide to leave the other? When we packed our suitcase? Several months earlier? Following an accumulation of differences and disappointments or emotional upheavals? When did we have the first idea of a breakup? When did the true picture that we had projected become too real? Was there an intuition that we ignored when we first met? To what extent is our desire for a separation conditioned by past love relationships? Is there a connection with the emotional wounds of childhood and adolescence? With our fear of abandonment? With the shock of separation during the experience of birth?

As we proceed with this examination, we will discover that we cannot find the moment of choice, whether for the great moments of life or for the simplest decisions. Why should I feel like putting sugar in my coffee today when I don't usually do so? In every situation we have to go back to the beginning of life.

The idea that we don't have a choice is based on the interconnection of everything. Since everything is connected, everything has an influence on the whole and conditions it. We are swept away in a gigantic whirlwind and transported to the unknown from instant to instant. Where would one then place a personal choice?

The absence of choice abolishes guilt, ours as well as others'. We can no longer hold the other responsible for our pain. He or she is being pushed by a force much larger than his own person or ours. Therefore, there is absolute freedom. Such a concept, however, is useless. It would only lead to additional internal conflict. So what can we do?

Look at reality, pay close attention to events, go with the flow of things then cease exhausting our strength in fighting against it. A profound joy emerges from that surrender. We can no longer pretend that we are in charge, that we can impose our will. We will allow ourselves to become sensitive to the creativity that opens up within us. We explore what is present rather than running after what is absent.

Interrogating our Choices

Take something simple, for instance, choosing a restaurant. Try to remember the moment when you settled on fish or meat, a dessert, a coffee or a tea. Was it while reading the menu? Or was your choice connected to previous food preferences?

Do you need to go back to your childhood to find the source of your choices?

If one of your choices is conditioned, how about the others?

Think about one of your romantic break-ups: the moment you decided to leave your partner. How far back do you need to go?

If you feel that every action is the result of an infinite number of events of which you are totally unaware, were you really choosing or did you act as a result of these constant and indecipherable conditions?

If you did not choose, how could you feel proud or guilty about an action?

If opposites get harmonised at the cosmic level, isn't any action perfect?

Try to find an event that you consider as very negative and attempt to see if nothing positive came out of it.

Do the same with a positive event.

6.

Looking for the Truth

WE SPEND AN IMPORTANT PART of our lives looking for the truth. But which truth? The one people try to impose on us through education, morality, religion or spiritual practices? Or the one we discover by ourselves? Does truth exist? If it did, it would present itself as an absolute that no one would be able to contradict. We rapidly become aware that no matter what our truth is, believers in different truths will be quick to attack it. Our efforts to make a solid and unassailable system are useless. No mental fortress can resist for long. We get exhausted seeking. We get exhausted defending. Is there not another path that would coincide with joy?

Huang Po, a well-known Chan master of the ninth century, goes straight to the heart of the issue by quoting one of his illustrious predecessors: 'It is useless to look for the truth; one just needs to not cherish opinions about it.' Every opinion involves a partial view. When we give up this view, the body-spirit calms down and relaxes, leaving room for joy. Huang Po adds: 'Our essence is open like space, that's all.'

A large part of our mental agitation stems from our imperious desire to find the truth. It is as if we were trying to isolate a star in the sky, so that we could give it the status of Absolute Star. Obtaining wisdom is to float: to not cling on to the opinions of others but not focussing on our own. Thoughts become more fluid; they pass by without encrusting themselves. The body looks at them with the same sense of wonderment as when it looks at space. Any mental and bodily tension prevents joy from becoming manifest. In order to arise, joy needs the openness of both the spirit and the body.

What is Left When We Abandon our Truth?

In my relationships with others, what is the part of my discourse that attempts to impose my truth?

In what way do conflicting truths constrain me?

What is the connection between my ability to listen and the abandonment of my fixed ideas?

What happens when I replace the word 'truth' with the word 'authenticity'? And what if everything were true?

7.

Spontaneity

and Fear

SPONTANEITY IS AN IMMEDIATE RESPONSE to reality. It implies having a body freed of its tensions, breathing naturally with a mind at peace, without fear. It is difficult to achieve. It could be considered the ideal test to discover to what extent a human being enjoys freedom.

We can apply it to ourselves by noticing our ability to respond immediately to life in all its unpredictability. Spontaneous beings have discarded the different masks that have been imposed upon them, as well as the ones they self-crafted.

Hesitation denotes confusion. Here again, we need to trust our body for its capacity to provide a rapid yes/no response to situations. The body is unable to say 'maybe' or 'we will see'. It reacts immediately by opening or closing.

The mind, however, requires a considerable time lapse to reach a conclusion and thrust itself into action. The strength of its hesitation is often so great that it convinces us to wait and do nothing. The internal discourse builds and maintains this fear by presenting to us all the negative possibilities that we need to consider before we act. With time, we become frightened human beings who wait for others or for life to push us into action.

Fear stems from our internal discourse. When the mind is quiet, what remains is only an instinctive fear that can help save our life; it is a direct answer from the body.

The fear that interests us here is a psychological fear. The one we create whenever we face an unexpected moment in life. This fear speaks to us, conditions us and develops further thanks to our incessant internal discourse. We can listen to it and dismantle its construction in the same way we would dismantle the workings of a clock and see it shrink the longer we observe it.

Fear has a body. When we realise that we are the creators of our own anxieties, we can slowly attain the silence that allows for spontaneity. The more spontaneous we become, the more joy will come to the fore. It is a fundamental joy, stemming from our freedom to act without needing any special reasons, since the beauty of the world and of people manifests itself naturally in spontaneity. We are then able to relate with a multiplicity of elements that enchant us, without any need to own them.

This joy is an unconditional delight in the beauty of being alive and of appreciating the infinite inspiration of reality as a mirror of our own creativity.

What am I Afraid of?

Make a list of your fears.

Is it possible to reduce these fears to one fear?

*Isn't the fear of a boundless space at the source of
all secondary fears?*

*How long do I need to respond to unexpected circumstances?
During this elapsed time, how is the mind behaving?*

*Am I able to observe a conflict between the response of the body
and that of the mind?*

Which one is the most immediate?

Is the repression of spontaneity a social fear?

When I achieve spontaneity is it because I immediately trust my body or my mind?

If my ability to be spontaneous increases, am I also able to think more quickly?

Is there a difference between my body, mind and emotions?

8.

The Illusion
of Change

THE IDEA THAT CHANGE IS necessary is an illusion. From birth, we are conditioned to adopt the conventional attitudes that will help us become socially acceptable human beings, potentially worthy of affection, admiration and love. We rapidly get used to a system that favours appearance over authenticity. The message that we constantly receive from our parents, teachers and lovers is simple: 'You would be better if you were somebody else.' This constant criticism pushes us to pretend to be what we are not so we can enjoy some peace. We buy books on 'how to be'. We follow methods, we attempt to hide our inadequacies from others and soon our own censorship becomes fiercer than that of our external censors.

When we succeed, we become objects of admiration for being someone we are not. We comfort ourselves with the fact that we're not the only ones who lie. We casually call this the 'social game', but this game only distances us more from who we are, to the point where we forget who we are. With help from a therapist, we try to find ourselves again, so we can rediscover our authentic selves.

One day, by abandoning the various methods of 'change', we begin to get a glimpse of another aspect of change, one that is not an escape towards the fabricated persona we believe we are, but one that allows us to return to the root of who we really are. We develop a particular tenderness for this suppressed but vibrant being. By dropping the mask, we discover the extent to which our authentic self has been deprived of expression.

This coming back to the authentic self marks a decisive step towards joy. This being who has been there all along is simply waiting to be recognised and loved for who he is. He asks to be accepted in his entirety, with his shadow side as well as his light side, his reasoning, his craziness, his excesses and also his creativity, which will develop the more we acknowledge the true 'him'. The more he accepts who he is, the more creative he will be. This long journey back to oneself is the only change that makes sense. Without it, the access to joy is blocked by a picture of oneself that is both false and an illusion.

We may experience some fear at that moment when our authentic being emerges, not realising how this new state is contagious. It is possible that those close to us may be shocked at first, but it seems unlikely that they would not allow their own authenticity to emerge. This emergence will enable us to meet those who have the courage to be themselves and who also allow themselves to pursue such exploration. Even if we encounter obstacles, the immediate impact of this process of exploration will be the manifestation of a joy to which no one can remain indifferent.

Am I Really Different Today?

Look at a picture of yourself as a child, while at the same time looking at yourself in the mirror. Is it essentially the same face?

Make a list of the most important conditions that you were subjected to since childhood. What were the recurrent 'values' that people attempted to impose on you?

What efforts did you make to be that other being?

Were you able to satisfy those who asked you to change?

Did your failure to change result in frustration, bitterness or a feeling of indignity?

Have you already had the experience of perceiving your authentic self and of abandoning any idea of being someone else, a disguise, a social mask?

What sensation did you get from returning to your essence?

9.

The Power
of Desire

DESIRE IS OFTEN CONSIDERED THE enemy of harmony and internal peace. Bedevilled by religions, it remains this unwanted remnant, which tosses us about on the crest of waves unless we get rid of if. Desire is almost always associated with a hunger that accentuates the difficulty of completely satisfying it. Spinoza says that associating it with power offers us a new understanding. By observing desire, we can understand its dynamic hold on every human being, even if it is renounced, which also becomes a form of desire.

This poses a question: To what extent is desire essential to joy? It is possible to change the perspective that we are at the centre of the universe, pretending that we are the only ones who possess a conscience. Let us imagine for a moment that matter is charged with consciousness and that it beckons us so to respond to our desires.

We will then be animated by lighter movements and be touched by a certain grace. No more one-way street. Everything is movement. The world comes towards me, I welcome it. I lose the supremacy of the 'I'; I float in a sphere that desires me, a sphere where each atom is pushed to bind with me naturally. This is exactly the definition of a joy that has lost all arrogance. The joyous individual is a being who is sensitive to the fireworks of what is real; he allows himself to be skewered and penetrated by the colourful explosion of what is continuously born and extinguished. Instead of being driven to concentrate on the disappearance of an object into the distance, such an individual will concentrate on the constant emergence of multiple new realities. Joy helps us discover this open desire as vastly different from a process in which we invest all our hope in one object, thus limiting joy.

The power of the imagination reaches its highest intensity in desire. Let us allow it to function, since it is a foretaste of more to discover. Allow this process to develop, without rushing, by fully appreciating the images that we form. Let us imagine the taste of the fruit before putting it in our mouths. This apprehension in the dynamic process diffuses the fatal coupling of desire and possession and shows us that the most delicious possession is to give time to imagination. If the object should then escape us, we would not feel any frustration, as we would have already fully enjoyed it.

This way of exploring desire shows us that there are two dynamic experiences in this movement: the first places total energy on a single object and then is bereft from not possessing it or losing it. The second operates as a beam that always stays in contact with multiplicity. This kind of desire does not know frustration. It is satisfied the moment it arises. One could say that it is the desire of the philosopher, a desire that does not involve stress or strain, a desire in the form of a space that includes the world in its fragile wholeness.

As we continue to observe how we desire, we can also discover that behind each yearning hides a larger and secret desire to find the authentic and free self; this slowly gets detached from its past conditioning and fears and is able to explore life with passion.

What are my Strongest Desires?

If others do not give me that satisfaction, can I reach it by myself?

Make a list of what I desire the most in the world.

Are there elements on that list that I have already tasted, but which I would like to savour as real and by the real me?

Would it be possible for all my desires to be merged into one desire?

Which one?

Is the satisfaction of this desire dependent on other desires?

10.

What is Real?

IN ONE OF THE MOST iconoclastic sutras of Buddhism, Vimalakirti, a lay contemporary of the Buddha, managed to deconstruct the concepts of the most advanced monks. We find in his sutras some pearls of the Real, in the sense that we mean it here: 'Reality is free of characteristics, since it is not conditioned by anything.' Sengzhao, his Chinese commentator (384–414AD), adds: 'No mental consideration conditions it, not the shadow of any representation, nor the echo of a thought. Characteristics unfold as conditionings unfold: remove these, and characteristics are gone.'

What prevents us from directly capturing what is Real and from finding immediate joy when we meet it? The heavy burden of our beliefs and certainties. At the heart of Chan, one finds the command of Chinese masters who state that it is essential to rid oneself of the conceptual apparatus in order to seize reality. This includes, of course, our Buddhistic dogmas, such as the emptiness of everything. 'Our school has neither slogan nor dogma to transmit,' states Hongzhi. As to the method, it is simple: 'Clean the dust and the stains of subjective thinking immediately. When these are washed away, your mind will be open, light, limitless, lacking both centre and extremes. Completely one, radiantly luminous, it will shine through the universe, cutting off past, present and future.'

When we touch this radiance, we are touching joy. But how do we suppress this conceptual filter that slows us down and distorts our perception of what is real? We need a clear and constant awareness of our mental functioning, an immediate insight in to our habitual attachments, our rejections and of our habit of always establishing preconceptions. Our opinions end up forming a heavy mass that interposes itself between reality and our perception of it. Our tendency to transform the smallest element in a story, which gets inflated each time we repeat it, ends up creating a filter that prevents the sap and beauty of reality to flow, thus creating a narrative without the semblance of any instinctual insight. From Basho:

> *When facing the bolt of lightning*
> *sublime is the one*
> *who does not know anything*

A conscience that is distorted by our conceptual knots shows us the absurdity of the internal discourse that transforms a cluster of perceptions into a cheap novel in which we are the heroes. Our ability to describe reality will progressively become blurred until this haze disappears. In the future, there will be almost no filter left between conscience and reality, almost no commentary. We will become that space that leaves traces of light and joy whenever crossed by anything.

Immediate Reality

Try to live an event without naming it, describing it or comparing it.

Is there a notable difference of intensity regarding reality?

How does reality emerge in the internal silence?

What does it taste like?

Is the not knowing an obstacle to the intensity of the sensation?

*How does the description of a feeling kill the intensity
of the feeling?*

What is the connection between internal silence and innocence?

What is the relationship between innocence and creativity?

11.

Thoughts, Emotions and Sensations

THOUGHTS, EMOTIONS AND SENSATIONS SEEM to be three independent domains. It is useful to consider them as such when speaking about them but in reality the connections are too numerous. Each moment is made up of a thousand neuronal bridges that communicate thought, emotion and sensation throughout our whole body. It is the lightning speed of these connections that allow joy to manifest when our system is not invaded by rumination, discrimination and fear – the first two of these being caused by the third. A careful examination will immediately reveal the effects of thought on our emotions. Our body shows impact immediately. Every moment, our body is exposed to an infinite number of climatic fluctuations – blood circulation increases, our pores open, our internal organs contract or relax, our muscles relax or clench to form a barrier to contain the emotion.

Giving attention to the body is essential for accessing the consciousness of the effect and for following the impact of each thought and each silence. A silent thought, that is, a thought freed of any reassessment – since the first thought cannot be considered a handicap – immediately relaxes the body, and, now aligned with reality, joy manifests itself instantly in this body. There is sometimes confusion when we speak of 'no thought'. This does not mean that there is a complete absence of thought, but simply that there is no attachment, or particular value given to thoughts. They move across space like a comet, or a flight of migratory birds, leaving no traces, creating neither an appropriation nor a second meaning.

In the intimate experience of joy there is never a question to resolve or the need to control anything. It is a progressive dispossession, the simplicity of being, an innocence recovered through the magic of being present in the world. This presence, recognised by mystics, artists and philosophers, is a two-step operation. The first is the concentration on a single object. As a result, the body calms down, the mind is quieted, the breathing is restored. This allows the second step to open us to the direct experience of the Real. Meditation makes us cross these two phases, traditionally known under the names Samatha (tranquillity) and Vipassana (deep penetration). But meditation does not always involve a sitting meditation. It can mean a presence in the world. Almost every Chan master has commented with humour and sometimes with a chiding veracity that sitting meditation transforms its practitioners into a bag of rice. They point out that to stay in emptiness is an incurable illness. Meditation does not 'go anywhere'. It does not seek anything. It is devoid of object. It manifests itself as an absence of connection. It is only a space in which the Real can rest from the need to represent any particular object. Interior silence does not arise from meditation; it is its own manifestation and this silence allows for 'music' to emerge. Meditation is a state of alert creativity, of mental lucidity, which we exercise when we connect with the Real, and which finds its most beautiful expression in action. There is no need to withdraw from the world to fully touch life and experience freedom.

Observing Thoughts, Emotions and Sensations

Have I already undergone a body-space experience?

When my mind is silent, where am I?

When I am silent, is there a separation between the world and me?

What is the impact of silence on my body and my perceptions?

Do emotions emerge more freely?

Do they pass through me as they would in space?

Do they stagnate in the body, as if it were a container?

Is it possible to have an intense emotional life in a body lacking conceptual limits?

Am I able to think, feel and experience an emotion and to move from one to the other without involving others?

12.

Developing Presence in the World

B EING PRESENT OCCURS SPONTANEOUSLY WHEN an object
or a person captivates us. Our whole attention is then
directed towards a single object and we are able to taste,
feel, see, listen to and really touch what we are facing.
This pleasure of presence is nourishing, restorative and
brings us joy. It is so intense that, during childhood and
adolescence, we spend hours in this state of receptivity
and curiosity as we discover the world. As we accumulate
experience and knowledge, our curiosity and sense of
wonder fades with time. We already 'know', and little

by little we lose the ability to be present. We experience boredom and lethargy. Nothing surprises us. This is the condition of most adults, who also interpret the natural ability of children and adolescents to be in the present as meaning that they are distracted.

This erroneous judgment pushes us to believe that presence means distraction, diverting us from the direct experience of the world by forcing the child to conform to the opinions of others.

If we think back to the most vivid memories of our adolescence or our childhood, we will discover that they were moments of pure presence. Our natural capacity for concentration on novelty enabled us to contemplate a leaf, an animal, a shadow, the starry sky, the sea, without the least mental fluctuation during long minutes, even hours. These moments left an indelible mark, while we sometimes forgot the names of people who were close to us, sometimes even the shape of their face. If we met them twenty years later, we would not recognise them. But the leaf, the sky, the dragonfly: yes.

How can we find this state of presence again? By a multitude of short incursions into the Real. Ten or twenty seconds are sufficient. We must make a minimal effort to really take a look, to feel, to touch an object, then, after a short lapse of time, we can let go of being present to return to our habitual state of distraction.

If we consciously come out of being present, after a while we will get a clear signal that we have been unconsciously non-present. This practice is somewhat frustrating at the beginning, since we force ourselves to abandon presence, yet it is within everyone's reach as it requires little effort and a short space of time. It is very effective in developing presence for a very simple reason: presence brings us pleasure and we love pleasure. This pleasure, repeated several times during the day, will reveal that there is neither triviality nor repetition in our daily life. Even if we shower every morning, each shower is totally different from the others. Even if we drink the same tea in the same mugs, the experience is new every time. This discovery will make us content to be alive, will reconnect us and will dispel our waiting for some event that might not bring us pleasure or happiness. We will spend a lot less time fantasising about objects that we think make us happy. And this is a good measure of the quality of presence, since it allows for the disappearance of hope, a form of fear and an acknowledgement of our inability to be present.

Presence also enables us to come out of solitude. It gives rise to curiosity and interest in others. Presence is a rare form of beauty. Every human being is sensitive to it. It is like being in love. Did you notice how an unusual curiosity and interest are awakened when you are in love?

Presence has the same impact. One could say that presence is a state of loving that does not need a unique object. It is an opening to the many wonders of the world in a radiant mental silence.

Testing Presence

*When somebody speaks, do I listen or do I think
of my response?*

*How many seconds can I concentrate on a single action with
mental interference: drinking tea, showering, eating fruit,
listening to music, reading one page in a book,
looking at the landscape?*

Do I have the impression that I can hear my internal silence?

*When someone makes an unpleasant remark to me, how long
do I brood over the words I heard?*

Am I aware of my ocular movements? Do I blink often?

Do I sometimes have the sensation of my breathing, of the movement of my diaphragm, of the relaxation of my tongue?

When I am in a difficult situation, do I confront it or do I try to distract myself in order to forget it?

When someone asks me a question, or when an action needs a reaction, how long does it take for me to answer or to act?

Are my answers clear or do they denote a lack of spontaneity?

Do I have the impression that I taste the small things in life, or am I always waiting for important events to which I attribute the power of changing my life and bringing me happiness?

Can I say that life offers me a lot?

Do I sometimes feel that my body and my mind are in perfect harmony?

When they are in opposition, which one makes the decision?

When I follow my instincts or my intuition, is the response faster than when I am in my usual mental space?

If I were more spontaneous, would I create more chaos or more harmony around myself?

Which makes more mistakes, the mind or the body?

When I make a mistake, how long do I think about it and how long do the internal commentaries last?

Do I feel guilty?

Do I sometimes simply become conscious of my mistake and immediately recapture my mental silence?

When I am spontaneous, do I regret it?

*Do I restrict my capacity for life in order to
avoid hurting others?*

*If I relaxed my attention, would my freedom enable others
to be more open?*

13.

Joy, Towards a Greater Perfection

Antonio R. Damasio, in his essay 'Spinoza Was Right', wrote:

'One can agree with Spinoza in saying that joy (laeticia in Latin) is associated with a transition of the organism towards a greater perfection. Without any doubt, [this is so] in the sense of the greatest functional harmony, and also in the sense of increased power and freedom.'

This functional harmony arises from a deep acceptance of our unconscious processes. The acceptance of this internal alchemy means that a large part of our internal processes are directly correlated to our awareness.

Our consciousness unjustly appropriates the idea of choice, when in fact choice is completely subject to the mystery and whims of the mind. What we call conscious choice is only a belated validation of a thousand unconscious operations.

Neurobiologists affirm that the brain needs only 23 hundredths of a second to carry out the operations that precede action and that the conscious part of the brain only chooses what the unconscious has already chosen. This sheds light on the inordinate pride we hold about the idea of choice. Our consciousness only then reaches a conclusion and in the best moments of spontaneity this happens seven or eight seconds later. In this case, spontaneity would only be the immediate acceptance of unconscious choices, without a theoretical, moral or social opposition. One could almost say that to be spontaneous means to be unconscious. This is what we could refer to as Consciousness.

Through their knack of mental silence and concentration, some Zen masters or practitioners of martial arts succeed in substantially reducing their reaction times by seven or eight seconds. This is what comes into play in the formal encounters where the master proposes a koan to the disciple and expects an instantaneous response will decide the advancement of the disciple in meditative practice.

The story of the Chinese master Xiang Yan, who lived in the ninth century, is an example. He told his disciple: 'Suppose that you are holding on to a branch located near the top of a tall tree by your teeth, and that you cannot use either your hands or your feet. A follower comes by and asks you what is the ultimate meaning of Zen? If you don't answer it means you are avoiding the question. If you answer, you fall and lose your life. What will you do?'

More than one second of hesitation is considered evidence of confusion. It results in an immediate return to meditation. The beauty of this practice is that it is impossible to conceive of a good answer. Only spontaneity can save us and if the student is bright enough to provide an answer, the master will certainly riposte unless he is absolutely convinced.

Following this example and without needing to practice Zen or any other discipline, we can test our capacity to respond not only to questions that are asked of us but also to the spontaneous events in life that require an immediate response. This will give us a clear view of our capacity to be alert human beings.

The Effects of Joy

*When you are feeling joyous, are you under the impression
that you owe this joy to an important event, or do you feel
an organic joy independent of any factor?*

When the reason for the joy disappears, does joy stay in you?

What is the impact on the abdomen muscles and on breathing?

*Does your body experience a gentle vibration?
Do your facial muscles relax?*

Do you feel like smiling or laughing?

Do you think of something else that could bring you greater satisfaction?

Does your heart rate slow down? Do you salivate?

Do you experience the same signs as when you are in love?

Have you ever experienced blissfulness without being in love with someone?

Do you have the impression that the body extends beyond its boundaries, that it dilates and fluctuates?

19.

A Balance

Between Automatic

Pilot and

Consciousness

I S IT POSSIBLE TO BECOME completely conscious? The multiplicity and speed of our unconscious processes is such that our consciousness would probably implode if we had that possibility. Is it also possible to avoid being absent to such an extreme that we can spend hours and whole days on automatic pilot? For our ultimate well-being and the blossoming of joy, certainly not. We can achieve a balance between these two extremities and, without getting tired or tense, we can slowly advance on the territory of unconsciousness.

We can gain access to creativity by observing our daily routines. Why do we have the need to respond endlessly in the same manner to the same situations? For instance, the habit of saying 'no' to anything that keeps us in our comfort zone. We are not risking anything by doing that since all the givens are known and under control. The 'no' is the guardian of our security and the guarantor of our ultimate boredom. It gives us the time to engage in our favourite occupation, the criticism and denigration of others, of their boldness, their errors and their follies.

The problem is not so much our inclination to repeat our actions, but the fact that we are not conscious of them. A habit of which we are conscious is on its way to disintegration. We often worry that others programme us – our friends, lovers or superiors in the world of work. We gladly accuse them of making our lives difficult. If we look at this more closely, we will discover that we are almost the only ones imposing the control on ourselves, limiting the possibilities of change and creativity. In the final analysis, others only play with the limitations that we reveal to them through the frivolity of our actions.

The more joy establishes itself within, the more we will realise that it is inseparable from freedom. And the more aware we become and put an end to our defensive routines, the freer we will be. Joy also increases our willingness to take risks and the desire to venture into unknown territory. The body immediately feels charged by a quiver of excitement giving the sensation that everything is functioning at full efficacy. The body emerges as a vibrating instrument out of a stagnant and dull mass. We follow a new path without being disturbed by the beacons of warning posed by those who fear reality. We clear the unknown as if with a machete and even the wild beasts look at us with amazement. One who knows joy will not cease the exploration of the Real.

Taking Risks and its Consequences

Do you believe that you are taking risks in the professional, emotional or physical aspects of your life?

Are you ready to call your ways of thinking and doing things into question if someone shows you a better way?

How would you welcome the change?
In your emotional life?

In your relationships?

Do you leave enough space for others so that they can modify their vision of things, their way of acting or thinking?

When you are about to engage in a new behaviour, does your mind present you with negative prospects about this change?

Or is it silent and allows you to enter immediately into action?

Do you expect that others will behave in the way that you hoped or imagined?

Would you say that your approach to life is creative, that it pushes you to invent and allow others to surprise you?

15.

Creative Joy

I F WE TURN OUR ATTENTION to the creative process of a painter, a musician or a writer, we discover that creation springs up during a state of mental silence, when everything that does not need to be thought is allowed to arise. A classical Chinese painter once built a studio for himself in the shape of a boat: A bunk with a slit for his arm was hanging on top of the paper, at the height of his stretched out arm extended by the brush. As he allowed the boat to float according to the capricious movements of the river, he would let go of his arm and his hand and the most beautiful landscape would emerge on paper.

Creativity is not the exclusivity of artists or of those who think they are able to inundate the world with their productions. It is accessible to all who discover presence and enter into a deep relationship with the world that surrounds them.

Creating one's life means constantly exploring reality and developing a greater acuity in perception, in refinement and in grace.

An artist worthy of that name always explores the unknown. He does not reproduce the work of others, nor his own. He is in constant movement towards the unknown. He does not pay attention to what others expect of him, since even he does not know where he is going. He creates so he can discover where he is by moving forward.

Let us see if we follow the same roads in similar situations. Habit always makes us take the same road. Changing our itinerary in a city can help us find new ways of behaving. We will become more conscious of the circular and obsessive routines, of the infinite repetitions of our gestures, words, thoughts, and physical sensations. The mind needs novelty, needs to perceive more and in greater depth, needs to not get used to anything, so as not to fall into a state of lethargy.

Sensory creativity is not repeating the same gestures or movements; it introduces different ways of touching.

Mental creativity means becoming immediately aware that we have already travelled along certain paths; attempting to open new mental paths whenever possible; becoming an adventurer!

Emotional creativity is not lapsing into the circular grooves that our lazy habits automatically present to us; letting oneself go; dismissing fear and mental foreshadowing; recapturing the innocence of the one who does not know.

Creativity slowly empties our memory, and an empty memory does not express a picture or a comparison to something else when an event occurs. Every moment is incomparable and of a luminous freshness.

Am I an Artist?

In your daily life, do you experience joy in creating something simple: a space for an object, a recipe, a sensory discovery?

How important is your contact with the arts: music, literature, philosophy, painting, sculpture. Does it bring you fulfilment?

Do you like to discover new creations?
Are you afraid of innovations?
Do you see creativity in chance encounters?

In your relationships, do you allow for creativity or a different approach, or do you feel more secure in repeating old patterns?

Are you aware of moments of wonder? How often?
In these moments, do you feel creative about what you observe?

Have you already had the experience of considering the
inanimate matter that surrounds you as creative?

Do you ever wonder if matter, the elements and the vegetal
and the mineral kingdoms could have consciousness?

Are you aware of the vibration of matter, of the dance
of atoms?

Do you sometimes have the experience of entering an ecstatic
moment, when there is no difference between you and what
you perceive?

16.

The Reintegration of Chaos

T HE FEAR IN WHICH OUR present society lives pushes us to forget about the creative aspects of chaos and to see only disorder and catastrophe. If we go back to Greek mythology, we will be able to see the creativity of chaos and then be able to reintegrate it into our lives.

Chaos was here before anything else, a kind of floating and undifferentiated magma filled with suspended energy. Then Gaia – the earth, sprang up, then Eros – love, Nyx – night, and Erebus joined and gave birth to the day and to the ether. Then love and hate appeared, to foreshadow the return to chaos.

By perceiving chaos as energy, we reduce both the fear we have of chaotic states and our desire to suppress our strategies to avoid them. Periods of chaos are marvellously creative. They are the end of a deceptively organised universe and bring the emergence of a new force. If we dare not to run away from chaos, and not to close our eyes, we will get the impression of floating amidst an ocean of a quivering energy. The body absorbs this energy, the spirit is nourished by it and goes through a phase of withdrawal and restful emptiness out of which the seeds of creativity germinate. It is the end of one order and the beginning of a revitalisation.

There is, in harmony, a sort of soporific softness. The desire to stay and settle in it is the simplest expression of fear. Piercing the harmony bubble to penetrate the chaos in which harmony seems to float is the beginning of a great adventure. Meeting with uncertainty stimulates our mind and body so paralysed by habit.

There is something suspect in our adoration of harmony. I can see a point in time in which an altar containing the statuette of Caesar, representing chaos, would replace that of the Buddha. Every morning we would present an offering of our abandonment of harmony by meditating on the beauty of the chaos that inhabits us, and its infinite possibilities. Situations are not chaotic, only our reactions to them.

Accepting chaos, floating on it as on a benevolent ocean, is a joyous state from which fear has been vanquished.

By ceasing our desire to control everything we will feel stimulated, encouraged to desire things to emerge. Control emerges out of the fear of feeling fully alive. There is no authentic joy without encountering chaos.

My Incursions into the Creativity of Chaos

Are you afraid of everything that seems like chaos in the arts, relationships, material matter or natural catastrophes?

Do you avoid coming near or opening yourself to chaotic situations?

Do you perceive emotional chaos as a danger or as a source of discovery?

Are you afraid or attracted to chaotic beings?

Do you resist that attraction?

For the last few years, our planet seems to be in revolt against our lack of ecological conscience. Do you experience this multiplication of natural catastrophes as a sign that we need to develop our consciousness or as a fatality?

Are you tempted by the idea of leaving your luminous side – the one in which you move with ease in order to explore your own dark side, the dark side of your desires, emotions and feelings?

When others tell you about diving into their selves and encountering chaos, do you feel like running away or do you feel drawn to such an adventure?

17.

Consciousness

CONSCIOUSNESS IS THE PLACE WHERE all the unconscious forces, all the cosmic influences and the activities of conditioning manifest themselves. To defend itself, it creates a moral consciousness and a consciousness of the world that revolves around an illusion of the unity of the 'I' separate from the whole. Consciousness is determined by a cluster of factors far too vast to be understood. The ego is the creation of this multiplicity that completely escapes analysis. Could there be another way to discover a consciousness that would not be conscious of any particular thing, one that would be an empty consciousness, spacious and luminous, that would include everything without a need to name it?

The practice of meditation, regardless of the form or approach, is able to reveal that awareness. Like the sky, it contains everything, where specific objects float like the stars. This meditation, where the one who perceives is at one with what is being perceived, is called Samadhi (a non-dual ecstasy). It provides a deep, essential and lasting joy.

This joy will help us understand that this infinite space is present in every object, every being and every particle of matter. One can say that this perception is the foundation of joy, since, like joy, it is not attached to a specific object.

We can compare this to a movie projector. There is the film, with the images representing the awareness one has of oneself, the moral consciousness, and the illusion of the ego. Then there is the light that has no form and is limitless, but reveals the frames of the film and gives them an appearance of continuity. If one were to remove the film, all that would be left is the light and the whiteness of the screen. But through the pictures, one can also see the light. To see the light of the film, one needs to know it before it gives birth to forms.

The Practice of Consciousness

Consciousness manifests itself as presence, and to work with presence is similar to learning a musical instrument, the body being our instrument. If we know how to develop our attention, it can harmonise with the world and vibrate spontaneously. In order to do this, it is better to practise many short exercises of fifteen to twenty seconds rather than a longer practice. Doing this thirty, forty or fifty times a day allows us to enter into deep contact with a sensation, like water streaming over our body, the contact of our bare feet on the ground, smelling and then tasting a cup of tea, looking at the sky, touching an object, listening to a bird, making eye contact with a stranger. Enter deeply into the contact, breathe by relaxing your abdomen, and after fifteen or twenty seconds, consciously leave this contact and return to your habitual mode. A few minutes later, choose another subject of attention and presence.

If you practise for several days, you will discover that the more your attention and presence develop, the more your pleasure of being in the world will increase.

It doesn't take long to discover joy. This discovery will cure you of waiting for an exceptional event that will make you happy. The more present you are, the less you will be hypnotised by hope. What is present, in this moment, in front of you, contains all that is needed to bring you joy.

The simple fact of being able to move, taste, feel, listen, touch and see is a miracle whose beauty escapes us too often.

After a few weeks, the body will desire more presence from you. It is an instrument of pleasure and, as it understands that there is immense pleasure in presence, it naturally returns to it.

You are entitled to live fully.

18.

Love

I F WE HAD LOVE WE would not need anything else and any problem would seem insignificant. Its scarcity sometimes precipitates a crazy impatience in us. Our desire for love freezes us and blocks our dynamism completely. We feel alone, isolated, in an effective coldness, with only the hope of being loved someday.

To receive love depends on others who can deprive us of it. There is a very simple solution that we do not always think about: giving love depends on us. To give love is, first of all, a manifestation of being present in the world, of the presence of the other, of the ability to listen in a state of physical, mental and emotional relaxation. Since we are not accustomed to others being present, it is natural for us to succumb to this absence that characterises our social relationships, leading to deception games, superficial connections and avoidance.

But if we give a few minutes of real presence and attention, the process of avoidance disappears. Presence calls for presence. We experience pleasure. An authentic communication flourishes. We are not far from love. When one gives, one receives. It is as simple as that.

In our love relationships, we often confuse gift and possession. A creative life implies that we give to others all the space they need in order to blossom completely. But once the enthusiasm of the initial connection passes, a restrictive process establishes itself: we limit the breadth of investigation of our partners; we want them to change, to conform to our ideas. Love languishes, changing to bitterness. We do not cut the wings of the other without paying a price.

Love is a constant creation. If we do not confine others within the limitations of our own concepts, if we do not freeze them in a picture, they will be able to evolve freely and, by appreciating their freedom, we will be able to rediscover them day after day. It is the only powerful tie that can establish itself between two human beings. All efforts to limit or control will result in the death of love.

In this reciprocal, creative bond, joy will manifest itself and bind people in a far deeper way than any promises and limitations.

Questions on Love

What is my definition of love?

According to this definition, would I say that I both give and receive love?

What is the part of possession in the love that I give to others?

Am I ready to give all the space needed for total fulfilment to the one I love?

Does this gift cover all areas: money, time, tastes, artistic and political opinions, and sexuality?

Does fear of abandonment have a place in my relationship?

Am I more generous in thought than in action?

Am I jealous when I love?

Am I jealous in life?

*Do I believe that the happiness of another person robs me of
a part of my happiness?*

*Is the happiness of giving love the same for me
as receiving love?*

*Have I already experienced a love that was not centred
on an object or a human being – a feeling of love that
included the world?*

19.

Body and Mind

I N Chinese, the same ideogram represents both body and mind. Westerners, familiar with a cultural and religious split, have a difficult time understanding this. To negate, even to torture the body is the way we choose to purify the mind. Unifying the body and the mind is the path to joy.

To find the body again is difficult. Giving up the constant internal discourse is even more difficult. The point here is not to negate the marvellous capacity of the mind, nor to devalue it in relation to the body, but to re-establish the right balance and stop making the body the slave of our thoughts.

What takes us away from presence is the constant and recurrent commentary of our desires, acts and mental fixations. If we could record a single day of mental discourse, we would have as much as fifteen to sixteen hours of continuous commentary of our actions and gestures.

By comparison, reading this book only requires an hour. Ongoing discourse is not life; it is only the commentary of a possible life that we do not really live.

By practising attention and presence, this commentary will fade and disappear. There will only be spontaneous action; no fear beforehand, no hesitation, no explanation after the act, but simply rest in the silence of the mind. This is what Chan practises and teaches.

Years of practice are required to achieve this spontaneity, but we can all reach a beneficial balance in which the mind, without being completely silent, will be able to generate open spaces, resulting in our actions becoming simpler and more direct.

To live in joy does not mean that we will be hypnotised by an artificial joy. We will continue to be sensitive to the fluctuations of life, but its manifestation will seem to be suspended in a space of joy. A body that is open and more fluid, along with a more open mind, will not cling to suffering, which itself will be dissipated in a relatively short time.

To reach a state of joy requires the courage to ask oneself questions and to answer them with authenticity.

The only goal of this small guide of internal navigation is to create a process that allows for joy to flourish.